The Floating Man

Katharine Towers was born in London in 1961 and read Modern Languages at St Hilda's College, Oxford. She has an MA in Writing from Newcastle University and lives in the Peak District with her husband and two daughters.

The Floating Man

Katharine Towers

PICADOR POETRY

First published 2010 by Picador
an imprint of Pan Macmillan, a division of Macmillan Publishers Limited
Pan Macmillan, 20 New Wharf Road, London N1 9RR
Basingstoke and Oxford
Associated companies throughout the world
www.panmacmillan.com

ISBN 978-0-330-51159-9

9 8 7 6 5 4 3 2 1

A CIP catalogue record for this book is available from
the British Library.

Printed by CPI Mackays, Chatham ME5 8TD

Visit **www.picador.com** to read more about all our books
and to buy them. You will also find features, author interviews and
news of any author events, and you can sign up for e-newsletters
so that you're always first to hear about our new releases.

in memory of my parents, always with love

The thoughts expressed by music are
not too vague for words, but too precise.

— FELIX MENDELSSOHN

Contents

The Floating Man

Amber

There's an element of truth
in its ancient atmosphere.
So precise, so frail a thought
to hold against the slipshod years.

First Word

for Lucy, found in Ethiopia 1974

Bedded in gentle blankets of dust
you're dreaming pictures of water
when the young anthropologist
kneels at the unstrung code of your limbs.
Three feet six but no child, he thinks.

You wear the constellation of your bones
as lightly as millions of years in the dunes
and let him caress with the pad of his thumb
the ash from under your arm, stroke
your loosening thigh from its sprocket of knee,

finger and breathe the flown cage of your ribs.
And what of this locket of pre-verbal jaw,
which soon must vouchsafe your first word?
Not *wheel* or *fire*, but one you've just learned: like *desire*.

Ash Leaves

The ash leaves fall when they're still green;
they fall in vivid heaps.
They clothe the ankles of the trees
and as they lie they weep.

For days they grieve and look back to
the ash tree's empty arms.
They miss the heights, the birds, the rain.
They wish the owl would come.

The ash tree shakes its brittle keys
and trembles in the wind.
How fine this winter life: bare bones,
the workings of the mind.

Pianola

This is the tune it has known all along
but kept in its puppeteer's chest of velvet and string.

The notes of Chopin's *Ballade* march out,
as if years of practice have put them
beyond the reach of mistake or expression.
The keys dip and lift, efficient as clocks,

and we notice the piano's reluctance to tremble or weep
as the signature dims into minor. When the *adagio* comes
there's no sigh, no blissful easing of fingers,
only a rickety pause that wants to be over.

With the last chord, the piano relaxes and shudders,
as if it has said what it meant, and none of it mattered.

The Art of Fugue

'Fugue must perform its . . . work with continuously
shifting melodic fragments that remain in the "tune"
sense perpetually unfinished.' – Glenn Gould

The violins pronounce their notes with care,
as if they are a question.
The flutes concur and answer in shy voices.

This is a beautiful subject. It bears repeating
by more solemn instruments, which yawn
and clamber to their feet: yes, they suppose they feel the same.

There's a sudden clamour of delight
that things could be so simple:
the clean white sail of a tune making everything good.

If they could find a way to make an end,
they would do it now, using their own words.

Counterpoint

If you and I could talk like this – your *basso
profundo* to my tricksy lilt –
we might invent a nicer line in argument.

It turns on centre of gravity: how the steady
left hand keeps the right from losing touch,
how the right must speedily elaborate

or qualify these stately declarations.
A mote of consonance might make an ending
we could set our sights on: my tune tangled

sweetly into yours as we pick our way
to the final, staggered chord. But you're still descending
as I climb up the bars, scrambling over flats and sharps.

We'll settle, then, for this ill-tempered truce:
you still banging away at the deep end,
me somewhere up in the gods, trying the high notes.

Planting Tulips

They might have thought I was praying,
knelt so long on the path; and truly
my hands were glad to be down in the dead earth.

Today a man was lifted from our bog.
He came out dark, shining like a length of flexed rope
and opened his inside-out eyes to the sky.

I would have said to leave him be
under the mosses and ling in the bog's orange juices,
not to take him from his own people.

I can almost forget which are my fingers
and which are worms trickling between them.
Perhaps I look like a beast run to ground,

or someone weeping. In spring
these tulips will come up black, stately.

Found

How strange and lost they are
when first we lift them up into the light;
old stones we've wintered in the earth
to learn the darkness underneath,
the patient needlework of worms
and how silence can spoil us.

I've half forgotten what it is
to turn their coldness over in my hands,
feeling for their openings and closures,
the roughness of their hidden, unmade places.
This word I hold is seasoned
to a gleaming bud of coal or jet,

irrefutable: one of the real things.

Starlings

The dark birds
seething down the winter sky
make themselves believe
they are a single soul
unravelling to a bald field.
They tilt and creak on stony ground:
hollow birds,
as if glory never happened.

The Dread

These birds have no weight but heart-weight.
They are all heart, borne by lightness

and space – space between feathers, and space
within their trinkets of bone. These birds

have no thinking, but know the curve and swing
of the earth, coasts where old ice lumbers and creaks

and why they must always forfeit the land.
They are mocking this scrag-end of beach,

all jitter and fret, telling each other
what they might know of magnetic north,

how small fishing boats are and how
the mother whales sing at night to the sea.

The Dread falls like darkness. It's as if
someone quietly said: *come, follow me.*

Dyad

If each note has its own appointed ghost,
let me leave behind this half-heard other
disappearing up the stairs as you approach.

I'll be the overtone, the quiet shimmer
in your mind when you're occupied
with some quite ordinary task,

the sudden spill of water down your spine
when you turn to close the garden gate
or pause outside an empty room.

You see, we're strung together in a chord of two —
you can't help raising me; I won't leave you alone.

Haunts

We can walk into woods and find
we are suddenly mortal.
The air has kept still for seasons
and we've no cause to speak

or to question this adequate moment
of moths, earth, light restrained by trees.
Let us not think we hear our own feet
treading the soft ash of leaves.

The Tuner

These days our piano doesn't sound itself,
each major chord or scale lapsing
into minor, each accidental
less a grace note than a fall.

As if your patient did not die
but might still rise and sing,
you dowse for buried harmony,
play *Invention No. 1 in C*,

try each strange chord, then try once more –
a reiki master tilted to your task,
growing bolder with each touch, and stronger.

As we wait, we hear each note
coming to itself in turn:
wayward souls, gathered home.

Coast

Only the high-born kittiwakes
have learned to pitch their lives
above the ocean's surly bass.

See how they step onto thin air,
calling their own names.

Pilgrims

They come on soft elbows, drawn
to a place to live as two dipped eyes.
They know why they come, and why,
when they're back, they won't sleep
but will sing, sing in the long dark.

In the Oak Woods

I waited to hear
the owls' late evening
call to prayer.

I lay down
under old-fashioned oaks,
quiet for fear the owls might startle
and fly from their rooms.

I waited to hear
the owls' late evening
call to prayer

and dreamed of moonshine
and moths, the sidelong
sidestepping fox who turned
to ask why I stayed.

I waited to hear
the owls' late evening
call to prayer

and lay all night
in old-fashioned woods
as the owls' pale faces
turned to ash in their rooms.

Violinmaker

He knows his tree by his fingers and ears.
Let fall, and he hears all its possible music:
tuning's irksome scrape and creak,
then a downrush of chords and glissando of leaves.

Bruinhilda

Split open my breast and you'll find
the tangled threads of a cormorant's nest.
For years I mistook it for my heart.

One day I felt the scuffle and scrape
of a long salt wing beating.

Camusdarach Beach

You also remember the ruinous sea:
the sky coming in from the north, and the cold;
the unconsoled gulls in the dunes asking *why*;
and the pool where we sat as diligent priests,
dipping and rinsing the souls of the dead;

the islands alighting at dawn on the water,
sitting like birds of stone
and weighing the light on their shoulders;
the seal in its shimmer of skin,
raising its orphan eyes to our gaze –
and perhaps, we thought, sensing our lives on the turn;

then coming back home, the waiting house empty
and closing its eyes to the sun.

Schiller's Apples

These days he asks for little.
On his desk, the windfall apples
Martha brings each morning from the garden.

The scent of Gravenstein
puts him in mind of something
his mother once said about dying.

When he lifts his pen, he hears
the old orchards,
their mild and tearful music.

Schumann's Bats

The garden frightens him.
At dusk the apple tree lets fall
its hoard of wings and tiny shrieks.

He'll keep his mind inside this room;
the piano's quiet company
will turn his thoughts to work.

He tries the keys: a melody begins.
Träumerei, soft-fingered dreams
of children not afraid to sleep.

The Chinese Philosopher

after Escher

I'm in that dream where I'm afraid to sleep.
I stand outside a room where there's a bed.
Its pillow has a hollow for a head.
Beside the bed, a book I've never read.

I find I'm counting sheep to stay awake.
Imagined sheep are dull, but these are real.
They nibble at the floor, making gloomy
little *baas* as they taste the trampled wool

then bundle down the stairs and out across
a field where there's a path towards a bed,
a pillow with its hollow for a head.
Beside the bed, that book I've never read.

I count the sheep again to stay awake.
(Imagined sheep are dull, but these are real.)
They nibble at the grass, making cheerful
little *baas* as they trot around the field.

Suddenly I'm on the bed – in the bed –
and dreaming that I'm sleeping with the sheep
which nudge me, making puzzled little bleats.
I dream myself asleep awake asleep.

The Dance

– *How long is it, my dear, since we danced together in the yellow field to Schubert's Impromptu No. 2 played loud on the wind-up gramophone? You were reading* Mrs Dalloway *and wanted to discuss its polyphonies of time and loss. Was it you or I who said we'd sooner die by the book than live like this? Later, when you stood to dress, I deliberately loved the angle of your shadow on the shaken stems. It might have rained. Did we dance again, and sing among the pelting drops?*

– *Please give it to me straight. Did you ever say you loved me? How long is it, exactly, since we danced?*

The Cello and the Nightingale

Seated nightly at her cello's loom Beatrice works each string,
bleeds her fingers to the bone to find and tell the garden's tune.

In a tree the nightingale unfurls the glamour of his song.
Is he the siren or is she? The garden shimmers in the dark.

Her melody insists and will not give. The bird sings on.
This head-to-head could last a thousand years.

Across the centuries they ply their dogged fugue,
rehearse – but cannot prove – the contrapuntal art of love.

Miserere

Never forget they are singing for mercy
these whey-faced castrati – and in darkness;
that every voice is no more and no less
than what it elects that day to make of itself.

Never forget that each altered version,
not written or kept, is a votive lit for princes and popes,
come to the chapel to wash their souls clean
in the voices of infants or immaculate men.

Never forget that plain song falls short
when God can be stitched in so many colours and threads
and the chalice of pride belongs to the voice

that decants bright C, and would have us believe
it is heaven distilled and dispensed.
Have mercy upon us, O God, in all thy great goodness.

Token

Up close and he's all there:
neat hands caressing the blind bend,
curved legs launching his blunt buddha's head.
Simple spirit of toad: I hold him up
between finger and thumb.

Machine

Re-ascending the oesophageal tract,
the capsule camera is already
committing to memory those starlit chambers
and soft, murmuring passageways

the staggered, iterative chant of the heart
telling itself to *beat, beat, beat again*
as the blood makes its orbit
of tissue and sinew and bone.

The camera can only tell so much.
Mostly we run on dark matter and trust.

Confessional

The heron steps onto the early air
as if he owns its greyness and its stillness.
He moves his wings on silent hinges,
sets the gentle angle of his spear.
He remembers raucous skies,
dark swamps simmering, and something more
that haunts his sleepless nights.
When he learns to pray he'll ask for
only simple things: a sudden dawn,
the attention of water.

Trust

At twelve, you still believe in the ocean
enough to swim naked,
darting through each green wave.

My deft little seamstress.

Stepping out across the million tiny bones
the sea gives up, you stretch your coral arms.
I can't believe you didn't drown.

Painting Flowers on Skye

for Winifred Nicholson

Still your flowers will not tell their colours.
The marsh marigolds you gathered on the shore
do not sing their note of feral joy.
Your irises stand cold as a bouquet.

Your painting is not art, but science –
the spectrum is an instrument where thought
finds ways to figure what we cannot see:
coasts of infra-red, *le rayon vert*.

You dream of yellow: lichen crusts
and lily root, brewed to the sting of urine
by soft-haired women in the crofts,
singing their Chinese singing.

Doldrums

Did you think you were losing your mind
when the notes took to moving
from under your fingers – slantwise –
and the wind went out of the high-blown
sails of Notre Dame?

The *Toccata & Fugue* gone cold
in the aisles, stopped notes dangled
from arches and pillars, and that hard-won
accidental left to hang in the roof
like a diagram of carbon.

Your ship stands silent in the water.
You rise to your feet,
scouring the distance for weather.

December

Being short of light and shadowless,
we are annual ghosts, and have learned to joke
that cheerfulness is mostly beyond us.

We make our own sense of things:
the caribou pacing the grainy dunes,
the tree's pale rigging marking the place

where there might be a moon. We sleep,
underestimate the dark, and when we meet
speak quietly; as if, close by, a woman dying

has woken to mouth a last word.
How can we live these run-down winter blues?
How can the restless sleepless herds?

Midnight Sun

There's no reason not to make a night of it again:
whisky and singing on the bright porch
while small-eyed whales lurch and moan in the bay.

These days, we've forgotten what it is to disappear
into our skins or walk under private stars,
our own idea of a moon –

and if we could only remember how in winter
we like to sit in a lamp-lit room
and turn the quiet pages of a book.

But now we live at a clear, sharp angle
and this polar tilt has us all on edge –
caught on the bright side.

The Whale

You came to find us, straying from your script
of deep thought and the sea's slow phrasings.
For centuries you swam alone through vagueness,
playing your oboe blues into the gloom.

You remember when the fisherman's net
was an angel's wing, gathering souls for boats,
and how your own surfacing
was like breaking the sun's hot skin.

Now your size is wrong among these rigs and lights
and you will surely die of all this vividness:
our stone-built brink where water ends
and the music runs out.

Double Concerto

for PB

Seeing your hand under his light arm
makes me think of Bach's two violins.

On the stairs you say you are too sad for music,
but there's a concert hush

as you steer him forward to the garden seat.
This is Bach: one violin takes up the tune,

makes us believe it's everything essential –
spirit, truth – then lets it lapse

so the other violin can know it too.
This is how it is: the tilt and sway

of melodies you share like oxygen,
breathing out, breathing in.

The Language Spider

I occupy an enviable position,
poised at the junction of the hemispheres
on my fingers of exact feeling.
I enjoy the best of both your worlds:
I can creep easily from one side to the other
and there's much to be learned
from these starlit crossings and re-crossings.
I know to respect the grave dumb-show
of your dreams and to favour stealth
over the grand gesture; I can crawl
into surprisingly small spaces.
Yes, I'm a clever little apparatus, stepping deftly
on my tenterhooks of anxiety and delight.
See how I inch this fragile, shining thread
down into the warm proof of your mouth.

Nightbird

Peel back my skin to the forest of bone
and listen at the latched gate.
She's there on a branch: don't startle her
from the humdrum lift and lapse of her song.

The Way We Go

the way we go about our lives
trying out each empty room
like houses we might own
eavesdropping for clues in corridors until

standing at a gate or attic window
seeing beauty in a flag of sky
we're gone, leaving the doors open
all the lights burning

The Floating Man

In this experiment of Ibn-Sina, I must float
for as long as it takes to forget the sweating desert
and the sifting streets of Hamadan.

No part of me may touch another body part.
My hands are spread so wide, each finger
thinks it is the only finger in the world.

My head is shaved, lest a stray hair
tickle my ear, or remind me that I'm beautiful.
I must take care not to hear my own heart beating.

When the time comes, you will ask me
who on earth I am. Shall I say a man or a thought,
or a man thinking about deserts and cities?

Sky folds me in. I'm as lonely as a spent star
calling into the darkness. Now ask again.

Notes

The Dread
the Dread: the momentary silence that falls before a flock of migrating arctic terns lifts into the air.

Miserere
In the eighteenth century it was *de rigueur* for those on the Grand Tour to hear Allegri's Miserere performed by the Sistine Chapel Choir during Holy Week. At that time the ornamentation was not written in the score but improvised, so that each performance was unique.

Painting Flowers on Skye
le rayon vert: a rare sunset phenomenon in which a ray of green flashes across the sky, just as the sun dips below the horizon.

Acknowledgements

Acknowledgements are due to the editors of the following publications where some of these poems, or earlier versions of them, first appeared: *Lit*, *Mslexia*, *Other Poetry*, *The North*.

'First Word' appeared in the pamphlet *'Slow Time'* (Mews Press, 2005) and 'The Dread' was first published in *Gift: A Chapbook for Seamus Heaney* (Newcastle Centre for the Literary Arts, 2009).

I would like to thank my editor Don Paterson for his many helpful insights, Sean O'Brien for his stalwart support and fellow members of the Northern Poetry Workshop for their advice and friendship. I am also permanently grateful to Andy, Bluebell and Daisy for giving me the time and space in which to write.